# My First Story of
# Jesus

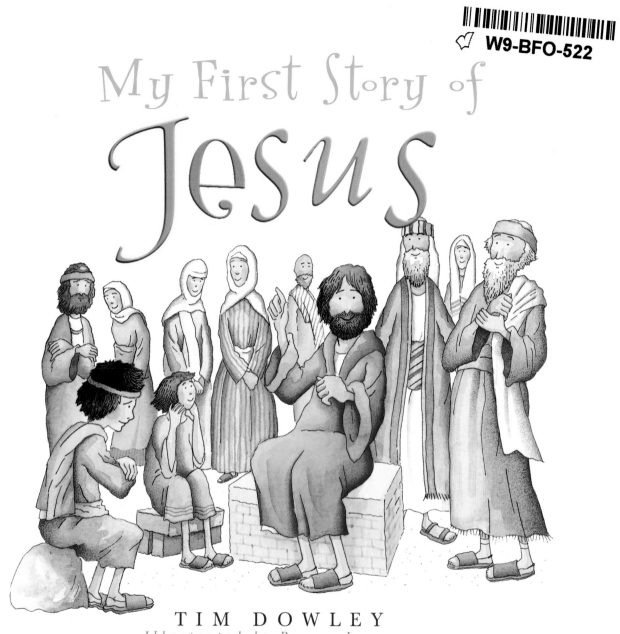

TIM DOWLEY

*Illustrated by* ROGER LANGTON

MOODY
PUBLISHERS

Jesus was born in a stable in Bethlehem.

Later, he went to live with his parents,
Joseph and Mary, in Nazareth.

When Jesus was twelve, his parents took him to Jerusalem.

But they lost him in the crowds.

At last they found Jesus again.
He was talking to the Jewish teachers in the Temple.
They were amazed at the wise things he said.

As he grew up, Jesus knew
that God had a special job for him.

Crowds of people went to hear a man called John
preach in the desert.

He dipped them in the river Jordan
to show that they were making a clean start.

One day Jesus came and said to John, "Baptize me, too."
So John dipped Jesus in the river Jordan.

When Jesus came out of the water, a dove appeared.
God said, "You are my son. I am pleased with you."

Jesus called twelve men to be his special friends.
Some were fishermen on Lake Galilee.

They visited little villages and big cities.

Jesus told people special stories about how God
wants our world to be.

People were amazed when they listened to him.

Many followed him.

Jesus told a story about a shepherd who had 100 sheep.

One day he lost one. He went searching for it all night.

At last the shepherd found the lost sheep.
He was so happy!

Jesus said that God is happy when anyone turns to him.

Jesus told the story of a man who was on a long journey. Robbers beat him and stole everything he had.

He cried out for help.

A priest passed by… A temple servant passed by.

Then a stranger from another country stopped and helped him.

Jesus said that the stranger who helped was a good neighbor.

One day Jesus was teaching lots of people in a house.
Some men came carrying a sick friend.

But they couldn't get into the house. It was too full.

The friends made a hole in the roof and lowered the sick man.

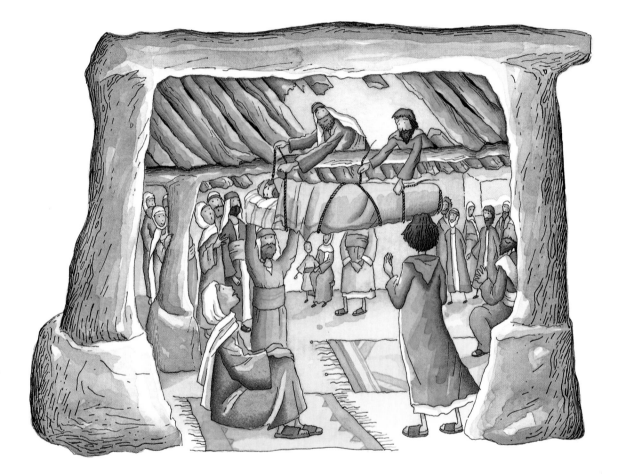

Jesus knew that they believed he could heal the man.
He said, "Get up and walk!"

At once the man stood up, picked up his bed and went home.

He thanked God for making him better.

One day, lots of people went into the country to listen to Jesus. They began to feel hungry. Jesus' friends said, "We can't feed them all!"

But one boy gave Jesus his lunch – five bread rolls and two fish. Jesus handed them out. There was enough for everyone!

A little girl lived beside Lake Galilee.
One day she fell ill. Her father went to fetch Jesus.
When they got back, the girl had died.

But Jesus said, "Get up, my dear!"

And the little girl opened her eyes.
"Now get her something to eat," said Jesus.

Once Jesus was sailing with his friends. He fell asleep. Then a great storm arose. His friends were very scared.

They woke Jesus. "Calm down!" he said to the wind and waves. And everything was still again.

Jesus of Nazareth was the friend of many.
He told great stories.

He healed sick people and did wonderful miracles.

But some of the priests hated Jesus
and plotted to kill him.

Because of them, Jesus was put to death on a cross.

But after three days he rose from the dead.

*And now he is alive for ever.*